How To Stop Being A Cheater

The Ultimate Guide On How To Stop Cheating In A Relationship

Michael Emily

All rights reserved. No part of this publication may be reproduced, distributed, or transmitted in any form or by any means, including photocopying, recording, or other electronic or mechanical methods, without the prior written permission of the publisher, except in the case of brief quotations embodied in critical reviews and certain other noncommercial uses permitted by copyright law.

Copyright © Michael Emily, 2024

Table of Contents

- Chapter 1 5
- Facing the Mirror 5
- Chapter 2 8
- Unpacking Baggage 8
- Chapter 3 13
- Taking responsibility 13
  - How to Be Accountable Following an Affair 13
- Chapter 4 16
- Communication is key 16
- Chapter 5 20
- Understanding Temptation 20
  - How to Resist the Temptation to Cheat 20
  - How to Remain Faithful Despite Being Tempted. 22
- Chapter 6 24
- Building Trust 24
- Chapter 7 26
- Developing Empathy 26
- Chapter 8 28
- Fostering Healthy Relationships 28
- Conclusion 31
  - Self-Reflection and Accountability 31
  - The Emotional Toll of Cheating on Your Partner 31

Identifying Reasons for Your Actions 32
Accept Responsibility and Move Toward Change
.... 33
Deciding Whether to Reveal The Truth 33
The Emotional Journey of Confession. 35
Identifying the Right Time for Self-Care 36

Chapter 1

Facing the Mirror

Cheating in relationships is a difficult and frequently emotionally charged topic that has sparked numerous conversations, debates, and research. While it is important to remember that each individual and relationship is unique, there are certain similar motivations and variables that can throw light on why some people choose to cheat.

It is the ultimate interpersonal infraction and a known relationship killer. The phenomenon, a popular chatting activity, is widely discussed but difficult to analyze. The goal is to avoid being detected, so why admit infidelity in the name of science?

However, scientists can provide new insight into a topic that is sometimes surrounded by shame and mystery. According to current studies, cheating is rarely a simple affair. There are numerous reasons why people cheat, and the patterns are more nuanced than popular clichés suggest. An intriguing new study provides some insight into these reasons.

The study comprised around 495 persons, 87.9 percent of whom identified as heterosexual. They were recruited through a volunteer pool at a prominent U.S. institution and Reddit message boards with relationship themes. The individuals acknowledged to cheating in their relationship and responded to the mystery's central question. An investigation showed eight main reasons:

- ***Low commitment***
- ***Need for variety***
- ***Neglect***
- ***Sexual desire***
- ***Lack of love***
- ***Situation or circumstances***
- ***Anger***
- ***Self-esteem***

These reasons determined not just why people cheated, but also how long they did so, their sexual pleasure, their emotional engagement in the affair, and whether their primary relationship ended as a result.

Though most cheating involves sex, it is rarely about sex alone. Most participants had some emotional attachment to their affair partner, but it was much higher in those who reported neglect or a lack of affection in their primary relationship. Approximately 62.8% acknowledged displaying fondness for their new companion. And approximately 61.2% engaged in sexually explicit communication with them. Approximately 37.6 percent had intimate chats, with 11.1 percent saying, "I love you."

Those who reported feeling less attached to their primary partner reported more emotional intimacy in the affair, maybe as a means of meeting that need. Similarly, when adultery was related to a lack of love, people considered it more cognitively and emotionally rewarding.

Participants' enjoyment of sex varied according to the cause of their affair. When someone betrayed them out of need for variety, lack of affection, or desire, they claimed to feel more sexually fulfilled. Those who named a scenario as the principal cause were far less satisfied. Kissing and snuggling were the most common forms of sexual behavior. In reality, the study discovered that just half of the cheaters engaged in vaginal intercourse.

The motive for the infidelity has a significant impact on its longevity. In some situations, the relationship was short-lived, while in others it lasted longer and became more intense. Those who cheated out of anger, such as a desire for vengeance, a loss of affection, or a need for variety, had a longer affair, whereas those driven by the situation, such as those who were "drunk," "overwhelmed," and "not thinking clearly," ended it sooner. Women had lengthier affairs on average than males.

Ultimately, women were more likely than men to confess to cheating on their primary partner, with just one-third of participants acknowledging having done so. Those who admitted to cheating were more likely to have done so out of anger or neglect than out of sexual desire or variety. This demonstrates that their confession was made with the intention of seeking revenge and retaliation rather than to atone for their transgressions. Individuals who opened out about their affair were more likely to be in a serious relationship with their spouse.

While infidelity is usually done in secret, some cheaters were less cautious than others, possibly on purpose. Those who cheated out of a lack of love went on more public dates and expressed more public devotion for their lover. PDA was also popular among individuals seeking variety or wanting to increase their self-esteem. Situational cheaters, on the other hand, were less likely to cheat openly, possibly because they wanted to return to their primary relationship without being found.

Finally, the fate of the individuals' primary relationship was determined by the motivation behind the conduct rather than the act itself. When driven by rage, a lack of commitment, a lack of love, or neglect, cheating is more likely to result in the breakup of a relationship. It was also less likely to do so if the adultery was circumstantial. Surprisingly, just 20.4% of partnerships ended due to an affair. The same amount of couples remained together despite their primary partner discovering their infidelity, whereas only 28.3 percent did not. The remaining partnerships ended for non-cheating reasons.

Chapter 2

Unpacking Baggage

Going through difficult experiences as a child does not guarantee that someone will grow up to be dishonest, but it may increase the likelihood of cheating. What we witness as children, the issues we face, and the lifestyles our parents model for us all influence how we behave as adults.

A person is more likely to lie to themselves if they were raised by parents who were unfaithful, for example, as this could give them the impression that cheating is okay.

However, nothing is assured. And it is always possible to overcome trauma, neglect, and poor childhood experiences. We construct our own destiny, and we all have a lot of control over our actions. Self-awareness and the ability to analyze one's behavior and compare it to one's ethics help people to shift views and assumptions formed in childhood.

Therapy can be quite beneficial in these situations, both for the person who is more likely to cheat and their spouse. When we seek therapy to help us understand ourselves and process and heal childhood trauma, suffering, and confusion, we may then select how we want to describe ourselves. That means we can choose to have integrity, to be monogamous or not, and to avoid cheating.

Here are some childhood experiences that can make an individual more likely to cheat, especially if they haven't dealt with the challenges or traumas they encountered as children.

Witnessing Cheating
Children learn about relationships and their dynamics from the adults in their lives. So, if a person grows up in an environment where cheating is acceptable, scientists believe they are more likely to mimic such behavior as adults.

If multiple, important people in a child's life cheat on their spouses or significant others on a regular basis, especially if those spouses and significant others refuse to discuss, confront, or end the relationship, the child is more likely to accept infidelity as a normal part of romantic relationships.

They may believe that everyone cheats. And see no issue with doing so as an adult.

Being told to "never settle"
Parents frequently teach their children to strive for the best and pursue pleasure at any cost. However, while this is a great lesson for many elements of life, it can have a negative impact on future relationships.

Children who grow up believing they should not'settle,' must be happy, must not be dissatisfied, and so on learn that life is more about them and frequently do not develop the skill of establishing frustration tolerance or understanding the need of reciprocity and flexibility in their relationships. In maturity, when they do not believe they are receiving what they should from their relationship or when they require more adulation from the outside world, they can develop the belief that they deserve to have what they want, when they want it, and to go get it.

This might result in an inability or unwillingness to handle the ups and downs of a relationship, leading them to abandon ship or seek reinforcement from others when they become irritated. Of course, this may be remedied by being aware of their actions, but it is worth noting.

Being told that their feelings don't matter
When it comes to parenting, there is a delicate line between providing an appropriate amount of emotional support and providing too much or too little. Of course, receiving an excessive amount of attention does not necessarily result in a person being a cheater, but it does enhance the likelihood.

If a child grows up with an invalidating, overly emotional, or domineering parent, they are unlikely to believe that their feelings are important. In relationships, they may find it difficult to advocate for themselves and set clear limits and boundaries because they have learned that love is all about keeping your spouse happy. As a result of avoiding disagreement to the point of loneliness or feeling deprived in the relationship, this individual may eventually feel compelled to'steal' what they desire.

Instead of coming to their partner and articulating their need for additional support, affection, or attention, they may seek it elsewhere.

Witnessing divorce
If a child witnesses a divorce, they can almost probably recover and go on to have a happy, healthy relationship as an adult. A divorce, however, can have

a long-term impact on some children, particularly if their parents handled the split poorly.

Divorced parents might cause their children to lose trust in relationships and marriage, resulting in infidelity. In addition, adultery is a common cause of divorce, and lone parents may struggle to find new relationships. Children witness and learn from these interactions, and they frequently replicate them.

There is also the possibility that these children will grow up without seeing a solid partnership. As a result, the youngster may miss out on learning about the abilities required to preserve faithfulness and monogamy.

Being cheated on
As we all know, it is fairly normal for children and teenagers to have connections that are very important to them, despite their young age. And how things play out can have a long-term influence.

Even as young as elementary school, children can create connections that resemble marriage or exclusive love pairings. Even young people can experience betrayal in a relationship, such as discovering a 'best friend' playing a game with a child other than yourself, discovering that your 'girlfriend' went to someone else's house to study after school instead of yours, or discovering that your high school sweetheart has been kissing a classmate behind your back.

While some children handle these situations well, others may react aggressively. After experiencing betrayal, a youngster may develop the belief that they must cheat on their partner before their spouse betrays them. At this stage, they accept their partner's infidelity as unavoidable, and the question is not whether or not they will be cheated, but how they would deal with the 'truth' that their partner is unfaithful. Unlearning this tendency might be time-consuming. However, treatment can help them rebuild their trust.

Growing up with a "absent" parent
Growing up with a physically or emotionally absent parent can surely influence how a person views relationships as an adult. These traumas can lead to the development of a cheater because they violate a child's inherent demand for safety and normalcy.

Without that safety net, children may grow up to feel insecure themselves. When a kid encounters a lack of security, they may be forced to look internally, potentially leading to insecure or avoidant attachment styles later in life, or outward to others for validation to help restore a sense of safety and self-worth, which can lead to anxious attachment styles.

Later in life, these kids who did not know where to seek attention will have a more difficult time dealing with the stress that comes with long-term, intimate relationships. As a result, they may seek out affairs in order to feel better.

It is possible to overcome; nevertheless, the wonderful thing about attachment patterns is that they are not fixed; they can be altered by the entrance of a good connection. Cheating is unnecessary if you find a caring spouse, communicate openly, and attend treatment.

Going through a trauma
Understandably, any sort of trauma or abuse might result in post-traumatic stress disorder symptoms. As a result, some people may feel tempted to cheat.

A common side effect of PTSD is avoidance symptoms, which lead to a hyper-focus on situations of hyper-arousal, such as high-risk sexual experiences.

On a far deeper level, the survivor who is cheating is frequently consumed by internalized shame, which, if not addressed and dealt with properly, can only pull survivors away from themselves and their loved ones, increasing their likelihood of cheating.

That is one of the reasons why survivors of abuse must get treatment and understand that it is not their fault. This allows them to have healthier relationships as adults.

Death of a parent
If a child's security is endangered while they are very young, particularly by the death of a parent, it can lay the stage for dishonesty later in life.

Attachment disruption, along with poor childhood experiences, tends to make people more addicted and engage in activities that seem good in the moment but are harmful in the long run, such as smoking, drinking, taking drugs, and cheating. Similar traumatic situations include having a parent with a serious disease, being incarcerated, witnessing a parent's drug addiction, and so on.

Remember, however, that nothing is permanent. If any of these events apply to you or your spouse, it does not guarantee cheating. Going to therapy and discovering childhood memories like these can help you feel better and have a healthy relationship.

Chapter 3

Taking responsibility

The error of having an affair stains your relationship. It's bad that you can't just apologize and move on. Instead, you must deal with the remorse that stems from having injured your partner in such a way. Now it is necessary to reconcile, but how do you do so? How can you hold yourself accountable and show your partner that you are actually attempting to rebuild the relationship?

Accountability is frequently defined as taking accountability for your actions. When someone is accountable, they understand why something happened and accept the consequences. Furthermore, they frequently accept responsibility for the consequences of their acts and do not blame anyone else for the outcome.

However, in some situations, assigning culpability to yourself can be challenging, even if you committed a serious offense such as having an affair. Issues within the relationship may have prompted you to do so, and you may not have felt particularly guilty about the conduct. Until you harmed your marriage.

The truth is that you cannot maintain a marriage or relationship while having an affair if you do not accept responsibility for your actions. Affairs are rarely legitimate. Rebuilding your relationship requires more than just expressing, "I'm sorry." It entails exposing yourself to your betrayed partner and holding yourself responsible for your vices.

How to Be Accountable Following an Affair

You must take responsibility for your actions, and there are numerous methods to apologize to the loved one you have injured. Infidelity has harmed each relationship in its own unique way. It will take a long time to repair the emotional damage and rebuild trust and closeness between you and your spouse. Unfortunately, there is no way to predict how quickly the betrayed spouse will come back, but you must not give up. Accountability is the first step towards forgiveness.

Stop the affair
Obviously, ending the affair is the most crucial thing. If an affair is still going on, it is impossible to heal the relationship. Yes, it may be difficult to terminate the enchantment between you and the other person, but if you are afraid of hurting your spouse, it is time to accept responsibility for that hurt.

Follow through with your actions
You ended the affair and expressed regret by apologizing. Now it's time to show your betrayed spouse that you're telling the truth. For example, if you offer to do the dishes, you should actually do them. If you agree to share your partner all emails and text messages for their peace of mind, follow through. Do not become frustrated or impatient with your mate. They're going through a lot.

Remember, this isn't about your feelings. It is about rebuilding trust. About demonstrating that you can be trusted and honest.

Express Vulnerability
During this stage of reconciliation, you will most likely go to therapy together. When it comes to addressing the flaws in your relationship and the causes of the adultery, you will need to demonstrate contrition. Furthermore, you must embrace vulnerability. It is acceptable in therapy to open up and disclose personal difficulties. The better you and your partner understand not only the problems in your relationship but also in your life, the more likely you are to recommit and persevere during this difficult period.

Don't forget how your relationship began: by being there for one another. By supporting one another. Taking a minor emotional risk during treatment will allow your spouse to see how you truly feel.

Show empathy
A cheater who shows no regret is bound to repeat their actions. Problems in the relationship are frequently used to justify bad behavior. To be accountable means putting those difficulties aside and being open about how deeply you harmed your spouse. Instead of defending your affair for whatever reason, listen to what your partner has to say. Recognize the pain you created. Listen to your partner and their needs in order to get through this. Empathy fosters accountability.

The bottom line in this discussion of accountability is that repercussions always follow events. If you dodge such penalties and instead blame your previously betrayed partner, you are not culpable. To recommit to your marriage and support your devastated partner, you must do more than flee. You have to be accountable.

Chapter 4

Communication is key

When it comes to love & interaction in a relationship, both partners must be willing to reveal parts of themselves. Even if some people are accustomed to keeping their ideas and feelings to themselves, it is critical in a partnership to have open communication channels.

There could be two reasons why you are hesitant to communicate with your lover. The primary reason for fear of communication in love relationships could be fear of rejection. The second reason is because you are concerned about what your partner will say. Maintaining these fears prevents you from properly cultivating your connections. To avoid disputes in relationships, real efforts must be made.

To build affection
Love can be compared to a flower; if not properly cared for, it will fade over time. When some people fall in love, they rely on the emotional tingle inside to keep them going.

However, it fades with time, which is why people split up because the vibes have changed. Communication is essential for maintaining a solid relationship with your partner.

With open communication between you and your lover, it will be simple to remind each other of why you fell in love in the first place. If you put forth a lot of effort to communicate effectively, honestly, and openly, the odds of falling out of love are low.

To resolve misunderstanding
One of the reasons for misconceptions in a relationship is that both parties perceive circumstances differently; this is why communication is essential. A relationship without communication will result in arguments and animosity since both partners do not agree with one another.

Unfortunately, this lack of communication will prevent both couples from recalling why they are at odds, which will prevent them from coming to a mutually agreeable resolution. In a relationship, when there is good communication, both parties are more aware of one another's viewpoints and can therefore come to a compromise.

Get to know each other
Another important aspect of communication in partnerships is getting to know one another. Several associations were formed as a result of a single encounter. Some of them meet at a bar or a friend's party, hook up, and start a relationship without fully understanding each other.

When the relationship faces a crisis, it will be difficult for both sides to comprehend each other because a firm communication foundation has not been established.
The truth is that if both people do not know each other well, a relationship will struggle to develop. The primary way to overcome this problem is through excellent communication.

At this phase in the relationship, communication is the most vital aspect.

Here are 9 critical communication skills for any relationship in a research study. These communication skills contribute to efficient communication within a relationship.

It encourages both spouses to respect one another.
Respect is one of the solutions to queries like "Why is communication vital in a relationship?". Some relationships end because of a lack of mutual respect. We like commanding respect in a variety of methods, and our partners will only know if they are kept informed.

What may not appear impolite to one person may be rude on all levels to the other. As a result, it is critical to communicate well so that all parties understand when not to cross the line.

It prevents guesswork
If there is a lot of guessing in a relationship, it can fail because both partners will continue to do the wrong thing, irritating each other.

You won't need to make assumptions about any problems in a relationship when there is open communication. Additionally, it would support the growth of a happy marriage in which neither partner finds it difficult to comprehend the other's motivations. With this, your relationship becomes less complicated, and everyone is satisfied.

To build trust
It takes time to establish trust in a relationship, and one method is through communication. Trust cannot be developed overnight, but when both parties are always willing to communicate honestly and openly, it may be built over time. As you learn to confide in your partner about anything that is going on in your life, your trust in them grows.

With efficient communication, you feel safe in your relationship. You are also confident that your secrets are secure with them because you have grown to trust them in the long term.

It allows partners to assist one another
One of the most exciting aspects of having a spouse is that you always have someone to turn to when faced with a difficulty. When faced with a dilemma, it would be a disservice to yourself not to share it with someone, especially your partner.

You might be missing out on the opportunity to lean on someone's shoulder. It is crucial to note that facing issues alone might be challenging, especially if your partner is unaware. You may be emotionally unavailable and psychologically imbalanced at the moment, which might lead to disputes and other issues. On the other hand, informing your partner enables them to comprehend and care for you.

It is an effective mood booster
If you can't openly and honestly express yourself in a relationship, you're miserable. One of the aims of any successful relationship is for partners to freely express their views, thoughts, and feelings to one another without fear of rejection. This is the act that honest and effective communication activates.

When you share your delight with your lover, you have the luxury of improving your mood since the atmosphere gets lighter. A healthy relationship is one in which both partners follow through on the complexities of good communication.

To strengthen the friendship
Partners who do not communicate in a relationship risk losing love, care, and affection for each other. One of the most important aspects of a happy relationship is effective communication. If you don't speak with your partner, you'll lose touch with them, and the relationship will progressively deteriorate.

If you have practical advice that may assist your spouse to develop, it is preferable to talk with them rather than remain silent. When they are unaware of their flaws, they will continue to make careless blunders, causing problems in the relationship.

As a result, you must engage in dialogue with them and assist them in recognizing their mistakes. You should also ask them what areas they would like you to enhance so that the entire building process is not one-sided.

You'll learn new things
When you're in a relationship, every day brings new experiences. Some of these encounters can be useful learning opportunities for your partner. As a result, it is critical to discuss new dreams, ideas, plans, and experiences with your partner.

If you are in a relationship, you should like communicating with your spouse since it allows you to discover more about them. It also helps your relationship become stronger, as long as both partners are devoted to making it work.

Relationships and communication are inextricably linked since the strength of the communication defines the strength of the relationship. It is impossible to overstate the value of communication in relationships since it is one of the key elements that guarantee the long-term sustainability of the partnership.

There are numerous suggestions and techniques for improving communication in a relationship; if you are struggling to create better communication with your partner, keep trying. After all, practice makes one perfect.

Chapter 5

Understanding Temptation

Remind yourself that you're not alone if you've been feeling lustful and tempted by someone outside of your relationship. Temptations can naturally arise in any relationship, even when you and your partner are at your most content. The goal is to recognize these feelings and concentrate on resisting them in a way that enhances your relationship. This necessitates hard effort, devotion, and loyalty to your relationship.

Temptations in a relationship might arise for a variety of reasons. Perhaps you believe your spouse is not meeting your emotional or physical needs, or your personal inadequacies are leading you to seek affirmation elsewhere. Sometimes, as unfair as it may appear, you may simply be bored.

These explanations might assist you in figuring out the root of your feelings, even though they do not excuse giving in to temptations to cheat. When these emotions arise, you may be tempted to avoid or repress them out of guilt. Instead, sit with your feelings and investigate their causes. Be honest with yourself and consider what might be driving your desire to cheat. Identifying your temptation triggers is the first step toward effectively addressing and resolving them.

It also helps to remember that you are not alone and, being tempted in a relationship is not uncommon. Being in a relationship does not suddenly make you less attractive to other people. Feeling tempted to cheat does not automatically indicate a problem in your relationship; however, it may indicate that your desire to be with your partner is decreasing.

How to Resist the Temptation to Cheat

You can utilize a variety of tactics to help you fight the desire to cheat. Some include:

Work on strengthening your relationship.
Begin by reevaluating and prioritizing your connection. Ask yourself if you truly want to stay in your relationship. If the answer is yes, recommit to putting time and energy into your relationship.

Engage in activities that promote emotional connection and open communication to maintain trust. Here are a few suggestions to help you reconnect with your mate and strengthen your bond:

Plan frequent date nights and prioritize spending time together. Trying new hobbies or trips together can be especially beneficial if boredom is the source of your temptation.

Express gratitude for the simple things your partner does and strive to recognize their efforts. Surprise your sweetheart with small tokens of affection, such as a handwritten note or their favorite snack. These thoughtful deeds will serve as a reminder of your affection for each other.

Make time for meaningful interactions with your partner, and actively listen to their opinions and feelings. Be open and honest about your emotions to build trust and understanding.

Set boundaries for yourself
Set clear limits to assist you in avoiding situations where temptation may occur. Limit your one-on-one interactions with attractive people and instead invite your partner or a group of friends to join you. This creates a buffer that prevents yielding to temptation or placing oneself in a micro-cheating or cheating posture.

Strike a healthy balance between your relationship and friendships
Ensure that you provide adequate time and attention to your relationship without sacrificing your friendships, and vice versa. Strike a balance between these two forms of partnerships. If you have an active social life, discuss it with your partner and listen to their worries if particular friendships make them uncomfortable.

Develop healthy coping mechanisms
Having healthy coping techniques in place will help you remain devoted to your partner in the face of temptation. Practice awareness, stay in the present now, and concentrate on the positive parts of your relationship.

Deep breathing and meditation are two techniques that might help you stay grounded and prevent impulsive impulses.

Exercise, meditation, and writing can also help manage stress and negative emotions, making you less likely to seek comfort and reassurance outside of your relationship.

Focus on Self-improvement
In a long-term relationship, you may feel as if you have lost yourself. If you've been experiencing temptation and can't pinpoint the source, it may be time to reflect on your own personal development and well-being. This will help you establish a stronger relationship with both yourself and your partner.

Engage in enjoyable activities that will increase your self-esteem and happiness. Improving your sense of self-worth and addressing your insecurities reduces your need for external validation.

Prioritize your emotional and physical well-being to foster a healthy mindset and a stronger bond with yourself and your partner.

Talk to someone
When necessary, get assistance from your support network. Speak with trusted friends and loved ones who can offer a judgment-free environment. Talk to them about your difficulties and ask for their counsel and assistance. While they may not have every answer, they can provide useful outside viewpoints and assistance in navigating complex emotions.

If you're having trouble resisting the temptation to cheat, try seeing a mental health expert, such as a therapist. They can offer advice and help you build techniques to strengthen your relationship and fight temptation.

How to Remain Faithful Despite Being Tempted

When faced with the desire to cheat, remember that actions have repercussions.
Consider the potential harm you may inflict on your relationship and partner. Cheating undermines the trust you have and may lead to the end of your relationship.

Consider the life you want to create with your partner and keep in mind that adultery could endanger your ambitions. Reminding yourself of the long-term consequences of cheating might help keep you grounded and devoted to your relationship.

Talking to your partner about the feelings you've been experiencing can be beneficial. It might be challenging to talk to your partner about your feelings of temptation, but honest and open communication is essential to a healthy, loving partnership.

If you're experiencing a transient desire, discussing it with your partner may be unnecessary, as it may create more harm than good. However, if the urge is chronic and recurring and may have an impact on your relationship, you must discuss it with your partner. When you decide to speak, choose the appropriate time and place. Make sure you're both in a relaxed and comfortable place where you can concentrate on the topic and freely express your emotions.

Throughout the chat, be attentive to your partner's feelings and reassure them that you are committed to them and the relationship.

To resist the desire to cheat in a relationship, you must first be self-aware, communicate effectively, and commit to developing your bond with your partner. Knowing the reasons behind your temptation, developing techniques to fight it, and having open and honest conversations with your spouse may all contribute to a stronger, happier, and more meaningful relationship.

Remember that conquering temptation requires continual work, tolerance, and understanding from both parties. Working together and supporting one another allows you to overcome these obstacles and cultivate a lasting bond. As you focus on your relationship and engage in your own development, you will be better able to resist the urge to cheat and form a long-term, loving relationship.

Chapter 6

Building Trust

Regaining trust entails demonstrating that you clearly understand what your partner has felt and experienced, as well as repeatedly demonstrating that you are sincerely remorseful and willing to change and work hard to regain their trust, no matter what it takes. Before they will trust you again, your lover will want a lot of evidence that you are a sincere, trustworthy, and safe person to be in love with. Rebuilding trust entails rebuilding your credibility.

It is both a rite of passage and a healing path that requires patience, courage, inner strength, and time for both the betrayed and the betrayer to recover, rebalance, and relearn the dance of trust. Your primary responsibility during this process is to be trustworthy, consistent, responsive, and reassuring. Here are some important suggestions to help you do that:

Call when you say you'll call
Arrive home on time. Make yourself and your timetable transparent.

Allow your spouse to vent their feelings in private
This means crying about what you've done, asking you a lot of questions, passing judgment, and even yelling at you, all while you remain strong, and faithful, apologizing, and reaching out with compassion and understanding.

Find out what your partner needs
Do what you can to improve the situation between you and your partner.

Full responsibility for your actions
This entails taking a long, hard look at why you cheated and how to ensure you never cheat again.

Promises you make are kept
Your words, acts, and deeds must be based on entire and unflinching integrity. Simply put, you do exactly what you say you would do. No falsehoods. No excuses. No exclusions.

Practice affection, attention, and appreciation every day
Every day, express your love and appreciation for your mate in both major and tiny ways.

Repeat as necessary
From my professional experience, the sooner you accept that the path back from distrust to trust requires perseverance, patience, dedication, and time, the more likely you are to succeed in mending your relationship.

Cheating does not have to result in a divorce or breakup
On the other side of this disaster, you can have a more honest, healthier, and happier relationship. It requires two people who are committed to staying in, being strong, and working together. Keep hanging onto the greater picture that you'll both get through this, no matter how wobbly things appear at the present.

Accept that sometimes it will feel like you're taking two steps forward and three steps back. One day it appears that there is hope for John, and the next you're sleeping on the couch again. Prepare a plan to help you keep calm and focused as you manage the inevitable bumps, difficulties, landmines, and setbacks that will occur. Rather than being astonished and overreacting, be prepared to take positive steps.

When you or your relationship feels stuck and struggling, remember to pause and ask yourself, "How would love to respond?" If something irritates you or your partner, or it feels like a frigid iceberg has floated between you, or the subject abruptly swings from reunion to break up, do this: Lean in, look your lover in the eyes, take deep, long breaths, and say these words: "I love you. You're the one I desire. We are important. I sincerely apologize for the anguish I caused you and us. It feels scary right now, but we'll get through it.

Take it one day, one week at a time, and stick to the eight criteria. Before you realize it, your connection will become more intimate, loving, stable, and strong.

Chapter 7

Developing Empathy

The first step toward empathy is to let go of all of your denial. You must set aside all excuses and allow yourself to be sad since you willingly participated in the most devastating exploit that marriage can endure.

You must remove the excuse that your needs were not being addressed. You must abandon the argument that the other woman/man did not mean anything. You must quit avoiding the fact that you acted selfishly and willingly committed an act that could be the end of a marriage.

Here's a sobering thought. Most people would not go to the trouble of harming their worst foes in the same way as an affair damages your marriage. So, why would you treat your spouse worse than an enemy?

You must also let go of any illusions that make you believe what you did was 'romantic'. You must especially abandon the notion that if you had not been married, your unfaithful partner would have been your soulmate.'

It is impossible to recover from an affair if you believe you acted on a lost soulmate opportunity. In fact, hearing this from the unfaithful makes me want to spend the rest of my life vomiting on their face.

The truth is that a soulmate relationship can only be formed when something positive happens. If you believe in soulmate theory, which is based on spirituality, you must also believe in all aspects of soulmate theory. That is, God or "the cosmos" does not bring your purported "soulmate" into your life when you are married.

If you believe this, you are engaging in a highly damaging sort of denial. The universe as we know does not play dice with people's hearts. So, please do us all a favor and remove your rose-colored glasses. The other person was never better than your spouse, and he or she was never worth it.

I'm going to ask you to put yourself in your spouse's shoes. Another deceived spouse gives you some advice on how to handle this. If you are truly sorry, you will mourn for what you have done to your spouse, whom you swore to love, honor, and adore.

You will set aside your own sentiments and do everything it takes to make her whole again. Cheating is wrong, and you were wrong. You cannot explain or justify what you did. Whatever happened in your marriage or relationship is unimportant. Nothing, and I mean nothing, excuses cheating.

If you wish to empathize with your spouse, you must admit that you were completely wrong and abandon all justifications. But you must also understand the gravity of what you have done, so that you can truly weep, because you have killed trust, love, and, most importantly, the significance of all that you and your spouse have gone through because your actions have nullified the vows you made on your wedding day.

Only when you comprehend the harm you have done and look at it objectively will you be able to empathize with your spouse and begin to restore your relationship.

Chapter 8

Fostering Healthy Relationships

Healthy relationship features appear to be evident, yet the line between good and terrible might be a little murky. Your relationship with your partner should leave you feeling cherished and secure. Your partner is someone who encourages you and has fun with you. Everyone defines good partnerships differently, but there are several elements that all contribute to a successful union. These are some signs of it.

Mutual regard
Respect is a key component of healthy relationships. It is important to consider how you treat one another on a daily basis. This trait in a relationship enables you to be open and honest with your partner.

Respect for your partner entails valuing their needs, emotions, and viewpoints. You speak respectfully to one another, support one another, encourage one another, and respect each other's limits.

Spending Time Together
When you have free time, you look for ways to spend it with your partner. You are ready and willing to participate in activities that they like while still pursuing your own interests. You make time for your friend despite your hectic schedule.

Date evenings become increasingly vital as your relationship progresses, especially if you have children. Spending time alone as a couple strengthens your bond, boosts your self-esteem, and brings you closer. This is a positive relationship trait for people seeking a long-term commitment with someone who appreciates your company.

Open communication
What's the point of being with someone if you can't communicate? If you've ever been in a relationship where one person is unable to articulate their thoughts or shuts down emotionally or verbally at the first sight of disagreement, you understand how difficult it can be.

Communication is essential in healthy partnerships. You get to know one another through conversation, and the more you chat, the more you learn. This is also true for couples who have been together for many years.

Great communication allows you to discuss goofy or hilarious topics, personal recollections, or ambitions, as well as resolve arguments swiftly and respectfully.

Sexual compatibility

Sexual compatibility is a crucial aspect of healthy relationships. This is because sexuality is intrinsically significant in most relationships. To begin, a couple must have excellent sexual chemistry both inside and outside of the bedroom. Couples should have open discussions about their sexual expectations.

No two people are precisely the same, especially in their bedrooms. Everyone has individual wants, kinks, desires, and expectations. This covers how much sex both parties desire as well as what they require in order to climax. Unselfish lovers are excellent lifelong mates.

Support

Couples who support one another demonstrate confidence in their relationship and allow their partners to be themselves and pursue their aspirations.

Support is also necessary throughout the difficult times that every partnership will eventually face. Giving your partner a shoulder to cry on and enjoying life's small achievements will help both partners feel happy and fulfilled in their relationship.

Trust

Trust is a slippery slope in relationships. It is tough to obtain and almost impossible to recover if lost. Breaking trust might alter your partner's personality and behavior toward you. When you're in a relationship, you want to be with a person who will keep your secrets and always be truthful with you, have your back, and never let you down. When you trust someone, you know they are dependable. You can rely on them. Couples that have mutual trust feel safer in their relationship, both emotionally and physically.

Confidence

Both parties should understand exactly how the other feels about them. This will make them feel safe and desirable in the relationship, as well as promote trust and bonding. Having trust in your relationship will also allow you to address difficulties and communicate more effectively because there is no fear that your partner may end the relationship after a disagreement. You are both deeply committed to your relationship and will go to any length to make it work.

You like each other.
This should go without saying, but many couples love one another but do not like each other.

It sounds difficult, yet it is really frequent. You may adore someone for their traits and the way they make you feel, but you dislike their demeanor. You do not get butterflies or smile when you receive a message from them.

One sign of a healthy relationship is that you both like and adore each other. When you have anything to do or some free time, your friend is always your first pick.

Honesty
In order to establish an open and trusting relationship, both parties must be honest. This does not imply speaking unnecessary negative things to your partner in the spirit of honesty. It entails having open and honest conversations on difficult topics such as sexual dissatisfaction, life goals, potential boredom, or thoughts of adultery.

These are difficult topics to discuss with someone you care about, but persistent honesty will bring you closer together and provide comfort in knowing that neither you nor your partner will have to worry about the other violating their trust.

Maintaining distinctiveness
If you love your partner so much that you want to do everything with them, that's terrific. However, it is also crucial for you to retain your identity in a partnership.

This healthy relationship trait ensures that both partners continue to cultivate their other relationships, such as those with friends and family. This will provide for a diversified and fulfilling social life. It also enables both parties to develop new hobbies and friendships.

Conclusion

Given that you are now experiencing a range of emotions, you may be wondering what your next actions are or how to proceed. Keep in mind that this incident does not necessarily indicate the end of your relationship or that your bond has been permanently altered. When you and your partner can communicate openly and move ahead together, there are several measures you can take to heal the relationship and begin to rebuild the trust that has been lost.

Self-Reflection and Accountability

Understanding the emotional effects and repercussions of your actions is the first step after cheating. Consider the influence on both your partner and yourself. This requires you and your partner to take some time to process your emotions. Consider asking yourself:

- *Do you have regrets?*
- *Do you feel prepared to be held accountable for your actions?*
- *Are you willing to devote the time and effort necessary to repair the damage caused by your cheating?*
- *Is cheating something you think you might do again?*

It is critical to be honest with oneself during this period. Once you've answered these and any other pertinent questions for yourself, consider how this has affected your spouse.

The Emotional Toll of Cheating on Your Partner

Discovering that you have cheated on your lover can be upsetting and perplexing. It can be extremely unpleasant and cause deep feelings of guilt, shame, and remorse. It's normal to be overwhelmed by these emotions and concerned about the future of your relationship.

Cheating can have a serious impact on both you and your partner, disturbing emotional stability and causing a huge rift in your relationship.

This is where you must admit that you are most likely the primary cause of their grief and disappointment. If your partner is aware of the infidelity, they may experience strong emotions like anger, resentment, worry, despair, betrayal, hurt, and uncertainty, all of which are normal and expected.

Their trust in you, as well as their feeling of self-worth, may have suffered significantly. In some circumstances, this could even be an attempt at vengeance. Although it is tough, realizing that these reactions are normal might be beneficial. It might set the stage for you to accept responsibility and determine how to proceed. If you want to stay in the relationship, these are critical measures in healing and rebuilding after a betrayal of trust.

If you are having difficulty understanding your feelings or require objective guidance, try contacting a couple's counselor or relationship therapist for in-person or online therapy assistance.

Identifying Reasons for Your Actions

Why did you cheat? This is a vital question to ask yourself if you intend to work through it. Many people, both male and female, cheat. You are not alone, and you are not the worst person on the planet. Perhaps it was a meaningless one-time occurrence, or it had a deeper significance. While there is no set guideline for dealing with this, it is critical to understand why cheating occurred in your current relationship. Here are a few reasons why this could have happened:

- *Boredom*
- *Feeling underappreciated*
- *Body image concerns*
- *Lack of emotional connectedness*
- *Growing apart*
- *Impulsivity and succumbing to a temptation*
- *Low self-esteem concerns*
- *Response to a shift in attraction*
- *Sexual desire changes*
- *Long distance*

After you've told your partner about the infidelity, they'll probably want to know why it happened. Understanding why things happened initially might assist your spouse get clarity and kickstart the process of open and honest conversation. If you're having trouble figuring out why you cheated, you might want to talk to a couple's counselor or relationship therapist. Talking to a therapist can help you evaluate your subconscious ideas or motivations, address any underlying mental health issues, and process your feelings after infidelity.

Accept Responsibility and Move Toward Change

Knowing why you cheated is important, but admitting responsibility for your actions is also critical. This is an important initial step in the process of reestablishing confidence. Avoid casting blame on your partner, as your actions are primarily your own. The unfaithful partner should accept full responsibility for their acts, display a willingness to be held accountable, and begin mending their relationship with their partner.

It is not enough to simply list the reasons; you must also grasp the patterns that lead to your conclusion. It's frequently about exploring your personal ideals, emotional needs, and relationship relationships. For example, you may recognize that the adultery stemmed from a sense of neglect and undervaluation in your relationship. It wasn't just a flash of impulsivity; it signified unfulfilled emotional demands and a developing divide between you and your partner. Cheating rarely occurs out of nowhere, and understanding these underlying issues can be eye-opening. Introspection can be difficult, yet it is essential for personal growth and the mending of relationships.

Admitting to yourself that you made a mistake is difficult but necessary to move past cheating. Recognizing the harm caused by your acts and where they came from is much different from merely acknowledging the act of cheating. This realization can be a watershed moment for you, prompting true guilt and a determination to change.

Another reason why focusing on these characteristics is beneficial is that it might lead to self-forgiveness. We do not mean to excuse your behaviors, but to accept and learn from them. It isn't about absolution; it's about allowing yourself to develop and heal. Forgiving yourself is important not only for yourself but also for making relationships work again.

Deciding Whether to Reveal The Truth

Although telling your partner the truth is undoubtedly the morally proper option, you may be wondering what to do after you've strayed. Choosing to expose or conceal your adultery has both advantages and disadvantages, and it is best to assess your own unique situation before making a decision.

Revealing the truth can help reduce your guilt, but it may also place an extra responsibility on your spouse. What appears to be a key discriminant is the type of cheating that occurred and the underlying causes. This can help you select the best course of action.

A one-time incident
Perhaps your scenario is a one-time cheating occurrence that was fueled by booze. When determining whether to disclose a one-time occurrence, consider the long-term consequences on your relationship. Consider not only the immediate satisfaction of releasing guilt but also how this revelation may affect your partner's emotional state and your mutual trust.

You may believe it is best not to tell your partner because it was most certainly a mistake and would only harm them. However, if you choose this course, keep in mind that you will be concealing a deadly secret, which may have its own set of consequences. If you choose to do so, take advantage of this opportunity to contemplate how to solve the problem or prevent it from happening again. Remember that we are all human and can make mistakes, what matters most is how we learn from them and adjust our behavior in the future. A cheater isn't always a cheater.

If, upon thought, you realize your actions stem from a deeper indifference to your partner's feelings, demonstrating a lack of true regret or care, this indicates a different level of accountability. In such instances, telling the truth is essential. It not only addresses your personal integrity but also respects your partner's freedom to make educated decisions about their future, possibly releasing them to follow pathways more aligned with their well-being and pleasure.

An affair
If you cheated on your relationship, the scenario was not an isolated incident, and you were having an affair, telling your partner the truth is the best, however difficult, course of action. In the case of an affair, you made the decision to cheat on your partner several times. This indicates that there is a problem with your relationship or yourself, which should be communicated to your partner.

If you decide to confess to having an affair, your partner may react with disbelief, hurt, or fury. As part of the trust-building process, you should approach problems with empathy and be prepared to address them.

Consider speaking with a therapist ahead of time to obtain a better understanding of your emotions or to learn how to approach the subject with your partner effectively. You'll also learn what language to use to reduce the possible harm you'll give your partner, as well as how to move ahead.

Voiced suspicion
If your partner has expressed concern or suspicion that you have been unfaithful, it is critical that you are truthful with them. Lying about your adultery is likely to create more harm than good, and it might jeopardize the possibility of repairing trust or moving on from the affair. When confronted with your partner's doubts, realize that honesty is more than just clearing your conscience. It's the first step in what will most likely be a long process of repairing trust.

The Emotional Journey of Confession.

When faced with the decision to reveal adultery, it is crucial to consider not only the act of confession but also the emotional journey that follows. As previously stated, confessing is more than just unburdening oneself; it is the first step toward healing and rebuilding. This journey is about understanding and empathy on both sides. As you travel along this path, keep in mind the long-term effects of your actions on your relationship. It's about developing a basis for trust and open communication, which are necessary for moving forward together.

Establishing Open Communication.
Perhaps the most crucial aspect of repairing a relationship after cheating is maintaining a good relationship with your partner through open and honest communication. Be willing to share where you are, who you are with, and so on until a foundation of trust can be built. Recognize your partner's thoughts and feelings about the infidelity, and avoid setting expectations or time restrictions for regaining trust.

According to research, one of the leading causes of broken relationships is insufficient communication. With this in mind, it is critical that you communicate openly with your spouse about your feelings, wants, and expectations, as well as be open to hearing theirs.

Transparency and Boundaries
Rebuilding trust after infidelity is a gradual process that requires patience, consistency, and a sincere desire to improve. It's more than just talking about the occurrence; it's about co-creating an environment in which both partners feel comfortable expressing their emotions and concerns: sharing

vulnerabilities is the foundation of trust, and it's an essential component of long-term relationships.

Consider the case of Dora and John as an illustration. Following Dora's infidelity, they resolved to improve transparency in their everyday routines. Dora began giving specifics about her day-to-day interactions, which, while initially difficult to accept and implement, helped to rebuild John's confidence.

Setting limits can help prevent future problems. These boundaries, which respect both partners' needs and comfort levels, can promote a sense of safety and security. Dora and John believed that having clear limits for their social contacts was an important step toward expressing their commitment to one another and the relationship.

Emerging Stronger Together
The road of rebuilding trust entails not only enduring a difficult period in your relationship but also development and progress. It's an opportunity to review and enhance the basis of your cooperation. The good news is that partnerships that survive infidelity and trust challenges tend to be more meaningful and resilient than before.

You could even argue that adultery is the shockwave that forces your relationship to address underlying difficulties and rebuild on stronger, more honest foundations. It's not simply about going back to the way things were, but about giving the partnership a new DNA made up of mutual respect, greater emotional connection, and a fresh dedication to one another.

Relationship counseling and couples therapy can help you emerge stronger from this experience, whether you're doing it alone or together.

Identifying the Right Time for Self-Care

In the aftermath of adultery, it's easy to fall into bad habits, such as ignoring your own needs while attempting to repair the relationship. Imagine you're Sarah, who was continually brooding about the situation, losing sleep, and skipping meals. She understood that neglecting her well-being was not only bad for her health, but also limited her ability to contribute constructively to the repair of her relationship.

Avoiding Unhelpful Patterns
When you're overwhelmed, it's tempting to resort to unhealthy coping techniques such as overworking, ignoring your feelings, or isolating yourself. For instance, you might say to yourself, "I cheated on my romantic partner, girlfriend, boyfriend, etc." at first, and try to "stay busy" to get away from thinking about it. Only to discover that these behaviors exacerbate your emotional distress. Being aware of such inclinations and intentionally selecting healthy coping mechanisms is critical for your overall well-being and the healing process of your relationship.

Recognizing the need for self-care is the first step toward emotional rehabilitation. Even if you believe you deserve the pain because you cheated, this may not benefit you or your spouse in the long run.

Implementing Effective Self-Care Strategies
So, how can you look after yourself? While working to understand and overcome infidelity in your relationship, you should prioritize both your physical and mental health. Taking care of yourself is a great way to ensure that you are in a good enough state of mind to focus on repairing your broken relationship. Consider the question, "What am I in need of right now?" Self-care might involve:

- *Meditating*
- *Spending Time in Nature*
- *Engage in your favorite pastimes*
- *Eating healthful meals*
- *Getting enough sleep*
- *Spending time with relatives and friends*
- *Exercising*
- *Journaling*

Self-care is more than simply self-indulgence; it's a crucial component of your healing process. It helps you achieve emotional equilibrium and prepares you to confront the difficulties of rebuilding your relationship. Prioritizing your own well-being allows you to contribute positively to your partner's healing process.

If you find that, despite your best efforts, you are still confused about how to proceed, or if you and your partner are unable to reach an agreement, it may be necessary to seek professional assistance. This is especially true if these challenges are beginning to interfere with your daily life, communication is deteriorating, or you are experiencing mental health concerns. There are various different therapies available to assist you deal with personal and relationship difficulties, remember that it is acceptable to ask for help.

Made in United States
North Haven, CT
21 June 2024